Building Your Future in Construction

A Step-by-Step Beginner's Guide to a Career in the UK

Construction It Is CII

Building Your Future in Construction: A Step-by-Step Guide to a Career in the UK
Written by Daniel Szczesny for Construction It Is
Research by Daniel Szczesny

Disclaimer:
This book is for informational purposes only. While every effort has been made to provide accurate and up-to-date information, the author and publisher make no guarantees regarding job placement, certifications, or career success. Readers should conduct their own research and seek professional advice where necessary. The author and publisher assume no liability for any actions taken based on the content of this book.

This book may contain links to third-party websites for additional resources. The author does not control or endorse the content on these sites and is not responsible for any changes, services, or policies they may have. Readers should verify all information before acting upon it.

All trademarks, product names, and company names mentioned in this book are the property of their respective owners. This book is not affiliated with, endorsed by, or sponsored by any of the organisations mentioned.

Table Of Contents

Introduction

The UK's economy largely depends on the construction industry, which builds our cities, the infrastructure we use, and the homes we call our own.

Every project, from tall skyscrapers to energy-efficient homes, starts with skilled workers who make the ideas come to life.

In 2023, the construction sector contributed over £110 billion to the UK economy, representing 6% of the country's GDP. The construction business is very important to the economy; it employs more than 3.1 million people, this is 9% of all the workforce, which makes it one of the biggest in the country. On the other hand, construction isn't just about numbers; it also provides chances to learn, be creative, and make real progress.
Whether you like the idea of making things, coming up with new ways to use space, or working with cutting-edge technology, this field is constantly changing.

It can be overwhelming for beginners to enter the construction business. It's simple to feel lost when there are so many routes, jobs, and requirements to be aware of. That's where this guide comes in.

This book will teach you everything you need to know to take the first steps towards a rewarding job in construction with confidence. It gives you clear, useful information on:

The different ways to enter the industry, whether through apprenticeships, trade schools, or direct entry.

Insights into various roles available, from electricians to architects, plumbers to project managers.

Tips on how to prepare for your first job, including obtaining essential certifications like the CSCS card.

Guidance on career progression, helping you set long-term goals and build a future in the field.

This is more than simply a career beginning guide; it's also a tool to help you choose whether construction is the best fit for you. Although the labour is fulfilling, it comes with difficulties like physical demands, hazards to safety, and the requirement of adaptation.

While this guide is designed as a step-by-step resource for those new to construction, it also provides valuable insights for experienced professionals looking to expand their skills, gain additional qualifications, or explore new career opportunities within the industry.

Let's begin.

1. Why Consider a Career in Construction?

Construction isn't just a business; it's an integral part of society that builds the basis for modern life. Building a bridge, school, rails, hospital, or housing starts with construction workers making the plans come to life. If you're looking to work in a satisfying, hands-on job, construction is a great choice. It's stable, and there are many ways to grow.

A Growing Demand for Skilled Workers

The UK construction industry is experiencing a significant demand for skilled workers, driven by a combination of factors. From ambitious infrastructure projects like High-Speed 2 (HS2) to the government's commitment to building more homes and improving sustainability, the sector needs a steady influx of talent.

In 2023, the Construction Skills Network reported a need for over 250,000 additional construction workers by 2028 to meet national targets. This demand spans across all levels, from entry-level labourers to highly skilled trades like electricians and plumbers. For anyone willing to invest in their skills, the opportunities for employment are abundant and promising.

The Benefits of a Career in Construction

Construction offers more than just a job; it provides a fulfilling career with many advantages.

Job Stability: Construction work is often less vulnerable to automation than other industries. Buildings, roads, and infrastructure will always need skilled hands to bring them to life and maintain them.

Career Variety: With roles ranging from hands-on trades like carpentry to professional positions in architecture and project management, construction caters to a diverse range of skills and interests.

Growth Potential: Whether you start as an apprentice or in an entry-level role, construction offers clear pathways for advancement. With the right training and experience, you can progress to higher-paying and more senior positions.

Tangible Results: Few industries allow you to see the physical outcome of your hard work. Construction gives you the satisfaction of creating something lasting that benefits communities.

Teamwork and Community: Construction projects rely on collaboration. You'll work alongside skilled professionals, forming strong bonds and building a network that can support your career.

Construction Career Benefits

- Job Stability
- Career Variety
- Growth Potential
- Tengible Results
- Team and Community

Competitive Salaries and Earning Potential

The earning potential in construction varies depending on the role, qualifications, and experience, but it remains competitive across the board.

Here's an overview of average salaries for some key roles:

Electricians: £32,000–£40,000 per year, with opportunities to earn more through overtime or self-employment.

Plumbers: £30,000–£38,000 per year, with similar growth potential as electricians.

Bricklayers: £25,000–£35,000 per year, with skilled professionals often earning more.

Architects: £35,000–£60,000 per year, depending on seniority and specialisation.

Site Managers: £40,000–£65,000 per year, with additional benefits for overseeing large-scale projects.

Entry-level roles, such as labourers, typically start at £20,000–£25,000 per year, but these roles often come with opportunities for progression and skill-building.

Please keep in mind that the above figures can change depending on things like training, location, and job demands. For example, professionals in London or people with specific skills may be able to get better pay.

Additionally, people who work for themselves or put in extra hours may notice a substantial increase in their income.

To find out about the most up-to-date and accurate pay information for your area, you should look at local job listings, industry reports, or organisations that specialise in your field.

Final Thoughts

A construction job has a unique mix of opportunity, stability, and personal fulfilment. If you work in this field, you can see the effects of your hard work in a brand-new house, a cutting-edge office, or an important piece of infrastructure.

Some people might not like how physically demanding and hands-on construction is, but those who are up for a challenge will find a job that is exciting, rewarding, and full of room to grow. Because of the constant need for trained workers in the UK, the industry offers a clear path to success for those ready to learn, change, and take advantage of chances.

Construction has something for everyone, whether you want to learn a trade, oversee big projects, or help improve the world through innovation and sustainability. The important thing is to find your place in this broad field and start building your future.

The next chapter talks about the key characteristics and skills you'll need to do well in the fast-paced construction field, which will help you decide if it's the right job for you.

2. Is Construction the Right Career for You?

There are many great jobs and roles in the construction business, but it's not for everyone. Determine whether you possess the qualities, abilities, and willpower necessary to succeed in a construction environment before pursuing a career in this industry. In addition to discussing possible challenges and how to overcome them, this chapter will assist you in considering your suitability for a job in construction.

Key Traits and Skills for Construction Work

A mix of practical aptitude, technical know-how, and character traits are needed in construction. While training and on-the-job experience can teach you many technical skills, additional attributes will offer you a natural edge in the field of work.

Physical Fitness and Stamina: Construction work can be physically demanding, involving lifting, climbing, and standing for long periods. A reasonable level of fitness is essential for staying effective and avoiding injury.

Attention to Detail: Precision and accuracy are essential when recording things or following safety rules. In construction tasks, even a small mistake can have big effects.

Problem-Solving Skills: There are times when construction projects do not go according to plan. Being able to adapt, think on your feet, and come up with solutions is highly valued.

Teamwork: Most construction work is done in teams, so the ability to communicate clearly and work well with others is crucial.

Work Ethic and Reliability: The industry values individuals who show up on time, meet deadlines, and are dependable, as the success of projects often depends on each team member pulling their weight.

Willingness to Learn: Construction is constantly evolving, with new materials, techniques, and technologies being introduced. Those who embrace learning will have more opportunities for growth.

If you already have some of these traits, you're well on your way to being suited for construction. If not, don't worry—many can be developed over time with practice and dedication.

Key Traits and Skills for Construction Work

- Physical Fitness and Stamina
- Attention to Details
- Problem-Solving Skills
- Teamwork
- Work Ethic and Reliability
- Willingness to Learn

Challenges of Working in Construction

Even though there are many advantages to working in construction, it's vital to understand the difficulties that the industry presents. Understanding them might help you prepare and decide if this is the right career path for you.

Physical Demands: Many construction roles require strength and endurance. Repetitive motions, heavy lifting, and exposure to weather conditions can be tough, especially in the early stages of your career.

Safety Risks: Construction sites can be hazardous, with risks such as falls, injuries from equipment, or exposure to dust and chemicals. Following safety procedures is non-negotiable.

Irregular Hours: Some projects may require working early mornings, late nights, or weekends to meet deadlines. This can be a challenge for those who value a regular schedule.

Job Security: While the demand for workers is generally high, some roles are project-based, meaning there may be periods without work between jobs, especially in self-employment.

Construction Work Challenges

- Irregular Working Hours
- Job Security
- Physical Demands
- Safety Risk

Assessing Your Suitability for the Industry

If you're unsure whether construction is the right path for you, ask yourself these six questions:

1. Am I comfortable working outdoors in varying weather conditions?

2. Do I enjoy physical work and being on my feet most of the day?

3. Am I willing to commit to learning technical skills and qualifications?

4. Do I work well as part of a team, and can I take direction?

5. Am I prepared to prioritise safety and follow procedures at all times?

6. Do I have the resilience to overcome challenges, such as long hours or demanding tasks?

Questions to ask if construction is the right path for you	
Am I comfortable working outdoors in varying weather conditions?	☐ yes ☐ no
Do I enjoy physical work and being on my feet most of the day?	☐ yes ☐ no
Am I willing to commit to learning technical skills and qualifications?	☐ yes ☐ no
Do I work well as part of a team, and can I take direction?	☐ yes ☐ no
Am I prepared to prioritize safety and follow procedures at all times?	☐ yes ☐ no
Do I have the resilience to overcome challenges, such as long hours or demanding tasks?	☐ yes ☐ no

If you answered "**yes**" to most of these questions, construction could be a strong match for your interests and abilities. If you answered "**no**" to several, it might be worth exploring alternative careers or looking into less physically demanding roles within the construction sector, such as design, project management, or administration.

Overcoming Barriers to Entry

You might face some barriers when considering a career in construction, but most of these can be addressed with the right approach.

Age: You can start learning at any point, but you should think about the physical duties and working conditions of the field. Construction workers often have to work long hours outdoors as they do hard physical work, which might not fit with the comfort and security that older people value.
But age doesn't have to be a problem for people who are physically fit and want to take on the tasks. Also, some jobs in the industry aren't as hard on the body, like project management, health and safety, or design, so they might be better for people who are changing careers later in life.

Inexperience: Entry-level roles, such as labourers or apprenticeships, require minimal experience. Employers are often more interested in your work ethic and willingness to learn than in your background.

Qualifications: If you lack formal qualifications, consider enrolling in a vocational course (e.g., NVQ, City & Guilds) or applying for a pre-apprenticeship program to build your skills and credentials.

Confidence: Starting a new career can be daunting, but confidence grows with experience. Take small steps, such as learning about the industry and networking, to ease into the field.

Final Thoughts

A job in construction is not a suitable option for everyone. It requires hard work, the ability to change, and a dedication to safety and teamwork. But for people who do well in a fast-paced, hands-on setting, it provides unmatched chances to create, grow, and win.

In the following chapter, we'll look at the numerous ways to go into construction, assisting you in deciding which path is best for you - whether it's through an apprenticeship, college course, or direct admission.

3. The Routes Into Construction

One of the best things about working in construction is that there isn't just one way to get started. You can take a path that fits your needs, whether you're just starting out, switching careers, or coming back to work after a break.

In this section, we'll discuss the main ways to get into construction and help you decide which one is best for you.

Apprenticeships: Earning While Learning

One of the best ways to start a job in construction is to do an apprenticeship. They give you both formal and hands-on practice so you can make money while working towards recognised credentials.

How Apprenticeships Work: Apprentices spend most of their time working on-site under the guidance of experienced professionals. The rest of their time is spent studying at a college or training provider to gain technical knowledge.

What You Can Learn: Apprenticeships are available for nearly every construction trade, including carpentry, plumbing, bricklaying, and electrical installation.

Benefits of Apprenticeships:

You'll earn a salary while gaining experience. You'll graduate with industry-recognised qualifications, such as NVQs.

Apprenticeships often lead directly to full-time employment with the company you train with.

To find an apprenticeship, visit the UK government's apprenticeship website. You may also look for opportunities with organisations such as the Construction Industry Training Board (CITB) or directly contact some major construction companies.

Trade Schools and Vocational Colleges

For people who want to learn skills in a classroom before entering the profession, vocational courses at trade schools or colleges are an appropriate choice.

Course Options:

Vocational qualifications like NVQs, diplomas, and T-levels.
Specialised courses in trades such as welding, roofing, or plastering.
Foundation programs for those looking to develop basic construction skills.
Duration: Courses range from a few months to two years, depending on the level and complexity of the qualification.

Benefits of Vocational Colleges

Provides a strong theoretical foundation alongside practical training.
Allows you to gain certifications that employers value, improving your chances of securing a job.

Many colleges and training centres work closely with local businesses, which gives students access to work experience and possible job openings.

Higher Education: University Degrees for Professional Roles

Higher education is frequently the best path for people who want to work as architects, civil engineers, or quantity surveyors.

What to Study: Relevant degrees include architecture, construction management, civil engineering, structural engineering, and surveying.

Duration: Most undergraduate degrees take three to four years, with some offering placement years for hands-on experience.

Benefits of Higher Education:

Opens doors to senior or specialist positions.
Provides theoretical knowledge of complex topics like design, project management, and sustainability.
Many universities offer connections with employers and internships.
This path needs more time and money, but the long-term job opportunities and money-making possibilities often make it worthwhile.

Online Education: Flexible Learning for Modern Times

For those who need flexibility in their learning journey, online education has become a practical and accessible option. Many platforms now offer construction-related courses that allow you to study at your own pace, from basic skills to advanced industry knowledge.

Benefits of Online Education:

Flexibility: Study anytime and anywhere, making it ideal for those balancing work, family, or other commitments.

Affordability: Online courses are often more cost-effective than in-person programs, with no need for travel or accommodation expenses.

Wide Range of Topics: Courses cover everything from beginner-level skills like blueprint reading and tool use to advanced topics like sustainability, Building Information Modelling (BIM), and construction management.

Recommended Online Platforms:

FutureLearn: Offers courses in construction management, sustainability, and health and safety.

Udemy: Features affordable courses on trades, project management, and software like AutoCAD.

Open University: Provides professional and degree-level qualifications in subjects like engineering, environmental studies, and construction.

Coursera: Includes university-level courses on construction management and green building practices.

YouTube and Free Resources: Many creators share tutorials and tips for trades and tools at no cost.

Industry Recognition:

Some online programs, like those offered by City & Guilds or the Chartered Institute of Building (CIOB), provide industry-recognised certifications upon completion, giving your qualifications added credibility.

Online education will be especially helpful for people who are entering the construction sector later in life or who wish to learn more about it before committing to full-time training.

Direct Entry: Starting with Entry-Level Jobs

If you're looking to start working right away, direct entrance into entry-level positions is an option. Many building companies are willing to hire people with little or no experience as long as they show they are willing to learn and work hard.

Common Entry-Level Roles: Labourer, site assistant, mate (e.g., electrician's mate or plumber's mate).

How to Find These Roles:

Search job boards like Indeed, Totaljobs, or local job listings.

Approach local construction companies directly.

Check with recruitment agencies specialising in construction roles.(list of the agencies listed in Appendix 1)

Benefits of Direct Entry:

You can start earning immediately without needing formal qualifications.

On-the-job experience allows you to learn and progress naturally.

Employers often support further training, such as funding your CSCS card or vocational courses.

Direct entry is particularly well-suited for those who are practical, eager to work, and open to starting from the ground up.

Reskilling or Changing Careers as an Adult

Construction is an industry that recognises people at all stages of life. If you're thinking about changing careers or returning to work, various training options are available.

Adult Apprenticeships: Many apprenticeship schemes now accept adult applicants, providing a structured path into the industry.

Short Courses and Bootcamps: Fast-track programs in trades like plumbing or electrical work allow adults to gain skills and enter the workforce quickly.

Government Initiatives: Programs like Skills Boot Camps and courses funded by CITB can provide subsidised training for in-demand roles.

Self-Employment: If you've already developed transferable skills, such as carpentry or decorating, starting your own business or freelancing could be an option.

The construction industry values life experience and diverse backgrounds, so don't let age or inexperience hold you back.

The Routes Into Construction

- Apprenticeships: Earning While Learning
- Trade Schools and Vocational Colleges
- Higher Education: University Degrees for Professional Roles
- Online Education: Flexible Learning for Modern Times
- Direct Entry: Starting with Entry-Level Jobs
- Reskilling or Changing Careers as an Adult

Final Thoughts

There is a way for everyone to get into construction, no matter who they are or where they come from. Depending on your preferences, the construction industry has many ways to get started. You can get hands-on experience through an apprenticeship, learn in a structured way through vocational courses, get a challenging education at a college level, start working right away in an on-site job, or learn at your own pace through online classes.

The most important thing is to decide to learn and grow and take that first step. Each path gives you the chance to learn new skills, get certified, and eventually build a rewarding job in this fast-paced, constantly changing field.

In the next chapter, we'll walk you through the most important steps you need to take to get started in the industry. This will include how to make a good CV, network successfully, and get essential certifications like the CSCS card.

4. Getting Started – Essential Steps

Starting a profession in construction may appear to be challenging; however, with the appropriate preparation, it is a process that anyone can successfully handle. This chapter will show you what steps you need to take to start your career in the construction industry, from finding the right jobs to making a great CV and getting your first job.

Researching Roles and Finding the Right Fit

The first step to starting your construction career is understanding the wide range of roles available and identifying which ones match your skills, interests, and goals.

Explore Job Profiles: Learn about different roles such as electricians, plumbers, bricklayers, site supervisors, and civil engineers. Resources like the National Careers Service website provide detailed descriptions of various construction roles, including required skills and salary ranges.

Evaluate Your Interests and Skills: Consider whether you prefer hands-on work (e.g., carpentry or plumbing) or roles with more planning and problem-solving (e.g., quantity surveying or project management).

Talk to Industry Professionals: Reach out to people already working in construction to get insights into their day-to-day work.

Look at Growth Opportunities: Some roles, like electricians and plumbers, lend themselves to self-employment, while others, like site management, can lead to senior positions within large firms.

Taking time to research roles will help you focus your efforts and prepare for a career that aligns with your strengths and aspirations.

Creating a Standout CV for Construction Jobs

When looking for construction jobs, even if you have little to no experience, having a well-written CV will help you stand out from the competition.

Tailor Your CV to the Role: Highlight skills and experiences that are relevant to the construction industry, such as teamwork, problem-solving, and punctuality.

Include a Personal Statement: Start with a brief summary of your career goals and why you're passionate about working in construction.

Focus on Transferable Skills: If you're new to the industry, emphasise skills from other jobs, such as physical stamina, communication, or attention to detail.

Showcase Certifications and Training: Mention any relevant qualifications, such as first aid training or health and safety courses.

Keep It Professional: Ensure your CV is well-formatted, free of errors, and no longer than two pages.

Remember that construction companies want to hire people who are reliable and have a strong work ethic. Make sure that these traits stand out in your CV.

Creating a Standout CV for Construction Jobs

- Tailor Your CV to the Role
- Include a Personal Statement
- Focus on Transferable Skills
- Showcase Certifications and Training
- Keep It Professional

Networking Strategies to Land Opportunities

Networking is a powerful way to uncover job opportunities and connect with industry professionals.

Use LinkedIn: Create a LinkedIn profile tailored to construction, including a professional photo, a clear headline, and a summary of your skills and goals. Join construction-related groups and engage with posts to build your network.

Attend Job Fairs: Many local councils and trade organisations host job fairs specifically for the construction industry. These events are excellent opportunities to meet potential employers.

Engage with Trade Shows: Large industry events like UK Construction Week are great for learning about trends, networking with professionals, and even finding apprenticeships or entry-level roles.

Leverage Personal Connections: Let friends, family, or acquaintances in the industry know you're looking for opportunities—they might refer you to openings.

While networking, it's not just about finding jobs; it's also about learning from others and getting good business advice.

Obtaining Your CSCS Card

The Construction Skills Certification Scheme (CSCS) card is often a requirement for working on UK construction sites. It proves that you have the basic skills and knowledge to work safely.

Why You Need It: Many employers require a CSCS card as part of their health and safety standards. Without it, access to many sites is restricted.

How to Get It: Book and pass the CITB Health, Safety, and Environment Test, which assesses your understanding of construction site safety.

Apply for the appropriate CSCS card based on your role (e.g., Labourer Card, Apprentice Card, or Skilled Worker Card).

Where to Apply: Visit the official CSCS website to book your test and apply for your card.

Preparing for the test may involve completing a short training course or using practice materials available online.

Securing Your First Opportunity

With your CV ready, your network growing, and your CSCS card in hand, the final step is landing your first role in construction.

Apply for Apprenticeships: Many construction employers actively recruit apprentices to train for specific trades. Check sites like Gov.uk, CITB, and individual company websites for openings.

Look for Entry-Level Jobs: Roles such as general labourer or mate positions often require little experience. These jobs are a great way to get on-site experience and build your skills.

Contact Local Employers: Smaller construction firms are often willing to hire enthusiastic beginners. Reach out with your CV and ask if they have any openings.

Use Recruitment Agencies: Agencies specialising in construction can help you find temporary or permanent positions suited to your skills and goals.

Get the Full List of 160 Construction Recruitment Agencies in the UK!

Scan the QR Code Below to Download

It might take a while to get your first job,
but persistence is key.
With every application, interview, and link,
you get closer to your goals.

Final Thoughts

You need to take many steps to start working in construction, such as studying jobs, obtaining certifications, and making connections. This approach can help you find your first opportunity and succeed in this dynamic business.

We'll go into more detail about the many construction jobs that are available in the upcoming chapter, including professional and skilled trade roles, as well as how to pick a career path that works for you.

5. Exploring Roles in the Construction Industry

The construction industry offers a wide variety of career paths, each playing a crucial role in shaping the built environment. Whether you're interested in hands-on skilled trades, technical roles, or project management, there is a career that suits your skills and ambitions.

This chapter provides an overview of key roles in construction, detailing their responsibilities, required qualifications, career progression opportunities, and what a typical day might involve.

Skilled Trades: Hands-On Roles in Construction

Skilled tradespeople are essential for turning blueprints into reality. These roles require technical skills, problem-solving abilities, and physical endurance. Most skilled trades are learned through apprenticeships, vocational courses, or on-the-job training.

Electrician

Electricians install, maintain, and repair electrical systems in residential, commercial, and industrial settings. They ensure that electrical components are safe, efficient, and compliant with regulations.

Qualifications:

NVQ Level 3 in Electrical Installation (required for professional recognition).
AM2 (Achievement Measurement 2) Assessment (practical test proving competency).
ECS (Electrotechnical Certification Scheme) Card (required for working on construction sites).
18th Edition Wiring Regulations (mandatory for compliance with current UK electrical standards).
PAT (Portable Appliance Testing) Certification (for inspecting electrical appliances).
Testing & Commissioning of Electrical Installations (for ensuring new systems function correctly).

Typical Day:

Reviewing electrical blueprints and planning installations.Installing wiring, lighting, sockets, circuit breakers, and control panels.
Diagnosing electrical faults and carrying out repairs or replacements.
Testing electrical systems using specialised equipment to ensure safety.
Completing compliance reports and ensuring installations meet UK electrical regulations.

Career Path:

Progress to supervisor, site manager, or electrical design engineer.

Specialise in renewable energy (solar PV, wind turbines), smart home automation, or industrial automation.
Start an electrical contracting business and work independently.

Plumber

Plumbers install and maintain water supply systems, heating systems, and sanitation facilities in homes, businesses, and industrial buildings.

Qualifications:

NVQ Level 2 or 3 in Plumbing and Heating.
Gas Safe Registration (mandatory for working with gas appliances).
Additional training in renewable heating systems (e.g., heat pumps, solar thermal heating).
Legionella Awareness Certification (important for commercial plumbing).

Typical Day:

Reading technical drawings and planning pipe layouts.
Installing pipes, boilers, radiators, and drainage systems.
Diagnosing leaks, blockages, and faulty heating systems.
Testing water pressure and ensuring proper drainage flow.
Repairing or replacing damaged plumbing components.

Career Path:

Specialise in commercial plumbing, heating engineering, or renewable energy systems.

Become a plumbing contractor, site supervisor, or mechanical services engineer.
Progress into project management or start a plumbing business.

Carpenter and Joiner

Carpenters and joiners work with wood and other materials to construct frameworks, furniture, and interior fittings.

Qualifications:

NVQ Level 2 or 3 in Carpentry and Joinery.
City & Guilds Diploma in Carpentry.
CPCS (Construction Plant Competence Scheme) Card for specialist carpentry.

Typical Day:

Measuring, cutting, and shaping wood for roof frames, flooring, doors, and staircases.
Assembling and installing windows, doors, furniture, and decorative mouldings.
Reading and interpreting architectural plans.

Career Path:

Move into site management, furniture making, or restoration carpentry.
Start a carpentry and joinery business.

Painter and Decorator

Painters and decorators apply paint, wallpaper, and other finishes to enhance the appearance of buildings.

Qualifications:
NVQ Level 2 or 3 in Painting and Decorating.

Typical Day:

Preparing surfaces and applying paint or wallpaper.Mixing colours and selecting appropriate materials.

Career Path:

Work on commercial projects, high-end property decorating, or specialised coatings.

Plasterer

Plasterers apply plaster to walls and ceilings to create a smooth or decorative finish.

Qualifications:

NVQ Level 2 or 3 in Plastering.

Typical Day:

Mixing and applying plaster.
Repairing cracks and damaged plasterwork.
Working with decorative mouldings.

Career Path:

Specialise in decorative plasterwork or commercial projects.Move into site management or own a plastering business.

Bricklayer

Bricklayers build walls, foundations, and other structures using bricks, blocks, and mortar.

Qualifications:

NVQ Level 2 in Trowel Occupations.
Apprenticeship in Bricklaying.

Typical Day:

Measuring and marking out building foundations.
Laying bricks and ensuring alignment with spirit levels and plumb lines.
Mixing mortar and applying it evenly between bricks.

Career Path:

Advance to site foreman or construction manager.
Specialise in heritage restoration or high-end masonry work.

Professional Roles: Managing and Planning Construction Projects

Professional roles in construction focus on planning, managing, and ensuring projects are completed on time, within budget, and to the required standards. These roles require technical knowledge, leadership skills, and problem-solving abilities.

Professional careers in construction often require higher education, specialised training, and industry-recognised certifications. Below are some of the key professional roles, along with detailed qualifications, daily responsibilities, and career progression paths.

Architect

Architects design buildings and structures, ensuring they are functional, safe, and aesthetically appealing. They work closely with engineers, project managers, and clients to bring architectural concepts to life.

Qualifications:

Degree in Architecture (RIBA Part 1 & Part 2) – Required to qualify as an architect.
Master's Degree in Architecture (Optional but recommended for specialization).
ARB (Architects Registration Board) Registration – Required to practice legally in the UK.
RIBA Part 3 (Professional Practice and Management) – The final step before becoming a fully qualified architect.

Typical Day:

Developing concept designs and technical blueprints using CAD software.
Meeting with clients to discuss project requirements and budgets.
Consulting with structural engineers, quantity surveyors, and construction managers to ensure feasibility.
Conducting site visits to oversee construction progress and resolve design issues.
Ensuring compliance with UK building regulations and sustainability standards.

Career Path:

Project Architect → Senior Architect → Associate Architect → Director of Architecture Firm.
Specialize in sustainable architecture, urban planning, or conservation projects.
Work in residential, commercial, or industrial architecture.

Quantity Surveyor

Quantity surveyors manage construction costs and contracts, ensuring projects stay within budget while maintaining quality.

Qualifications:

Degree in Quantity Surveying, Construction Economics, or Civil Engineering.RICS (Royal Institution of Chartered Surveyors) Accreditation – Required for professional recognition.

NVQ Level 6 or 7 in Quantity Surveying (for those working their way up from site-based roles).

Typical Day:

Preparing detailed cost estimates and budgets for construction projects.
Conducting financial risk assessments and cost forecasting.
Negotiating prices with suppliers and contractors to optimize expenditures.
Managing project contracts and ensuring legal compliance.
Visiting construction sites to monitor progress and control costs.

Career Path:

Junior Quantity Surveyor → Senior QS → Commercial Manager → Director of Cost Consultancy.

Specialize in infrastructure, residential, or high-rise commercial developments.

Project Manager

Project managers oversee the planning, execution, and completion of construction projects. They are responsible for ensuring that work is carried out on time, within budget, and meets quality standards.

Qualifications:

Degree in Construction Management, Civil Engineering, or a related field.

NVQ Level 6 or 7 in Construction Management (for experienced professionals transitioning from site-based roles).
PRINCE2 or PMP (Project Management Professional) Certification – Recognised project management qualifications.
SMSTS (Site Management Safety Training Scheme) – Required for managing health and safety on-site.

Typical Day:

Creating and updating project timelines and schedules.
Coordinating with site managers, subcontractors, and suppliers.
Reviewing and approving construction plans and work progress reports.
Ensuring compliance with health and safety regulations.
Managing budgets, procurement, and resource allocation.
Resolving unexpected issues that arise on-site.

Career Path:

Assistant Project Manager → Project Manager → Senior Project Manager → Construction Director.
Specialise in large-scale infrastructure, high-rise developments, or commercial projects.

Construction Manager

Construction managers are responsible for overseeing daily site operations and ensuring that work is progressing according to schedule and within regulatory requirements.

Qualifications:

Degree in Construction Management, Civil Engineering, or a related field.
NVQ Level 6 or 7 in Construction Site Management – Required for leadership roles.
SMSTS (Site Management Safety Training Scheme) – Essential for managing site safety.
CIOB (Chartered Institute of Building) Membership – Recognised for professional development.

Typical Day:

Supervising construction teams and subcontractors.
Managing material deliveries and equipment usage.
Conducting regular site safety inspections.
Ensuring compliance with building regulations and site policies.
Liaising with architects, engineers, and surveyors to address site issues.

Career Path:

Site Supervisor → Construction Manager → Regional Construction Director.
Specialise in residential, commercial, or industrial projects.

Site Supervisor

Site supervisors play a critical role in managing the daily operations of a construction site. They act as a key link between workers, site managers, and project teams, ensuring that projects progress safely, efficiently, and in line with industry regulations.

Site supervisors are responsible for overseeing on-site activities, coordinating teams, enforcing safety protocols, and maintaining quality standards throughout the construction process.

Qualifications:

NVQ Level 3 or 4 in Construction Site Supervision – The most recognised qualification for this role.
SSSTS (Site Supervisor Safety Training Scheme) – A mandatory safety certification for supervising on-site workers.
CSCS (Construction Skills Certification Scheme) Gold Card – Required for supervisory roles on most UK construction sites.
First Aid at Work Certificate – Recommended for emergency response responsibilities.
Temporary Works Supervisor Training – Beneficial for overseeing temporary structures like scaffolding and trenches.
Fire Marshal Training – Often required for large or high-risk construction sites.

Typical Day:

Conducting morning briefings and toolbox talks to outline daily tasks and safety updates.
Supervising construction workers, subcontractors, and site operatives to ensure work is completed on time and to specification.
Monitoring site safety and ensuring compliance with health and safety regulations.Inspecting materials, tools, and equipment to ensure proper use and maintenance.
Communicating with site managers, engineers, and project managers to report progress and resolve issues.

Keeping site records, completing reports, and ensuring all documentation is up to date.

Career Path:

Site Operative → Site Supervisor → Assistant Site Manager → Site Manager → Project Manager.
Specialise in health and safety supervision, quality control, or logistics management.
Progress into contract management, construction site auditing, or training and mentoring new supervisors.

Engineering and Design Roles in Construction

Engineers and designers play a critical role in the planning, development, and execution of construction projects. They are responsible for analysing, designing, and ensuring the structural integrity, efficiency, and sustainability of buildings and infrastructure. Each discipline has a specialised focus, ensuring that projects meet safety standards, regulatory requirements, and functional needs.

Civil Engineer

Civil engineers design and oversee infrastructure projects such as roads, bridges, tunnels, and drainage systems.

Qualifications:

Degree in Civil Engineering (BEng or MEng).
ICE (Institution of Civil Engineers) Accreditation – Required for chartered status.

NVQ Level 6 or 7 in Civil Engineering Management (for non-degree routes).

Typical Day:

Designing and analysing structural components of infrastructure projects.
Conducting site inspections and supervising construction teams.
Preparing technical reports and feasibility studies.
Ensuring compliance with environmental and safety regulations.

Career Path:

Graduate Civil Engineer → Senior Engineer → Principal Engineer → Director of Engineering Firm.
Specialise in transportation engineering, water resources, or urban infrastructure planning.

Structural Engineer

Structural engineers ensure that buildings and structures can withstand forces such as wind, earthquakes, and heavy loads.

Qualifications:

Degree in Structural Engineering or Civil Engineering.
IStructE (Institution of Structural Engineers) Membership – Required for chartered status.

Typical Day:

Designing load-bearing elements like beams, columns, and foundations.

Using finite element analysis (FEA) software to simulate structural performance.
Conducting safety assessments and material testing.

Career Path:

Structural Engineer → Lead Engineer → Consulting Engineer.

Mechanical Engineer

Mechanical engineers work on HVAC (heating, ventilation, and air conditioning) and mechanical systems in buildings.

Qualifications:

Degree in Mechanical Engineering.

Typical Day:

Designing ventilation, heating, and cooling systems.
Conducting efficiency assessments.

Career Path:

Mechanical Engineer → Senior Engineer → Engineering Director.

Electrical Engineer

Electrical engineers design, install, and maintain electrical systems in residential, commercial, and industrial buildings. Their work ensures that power distribution, lighting, and automation systems are efficient, safe, and compliant with regulations. They play a crucial role in integrating renewable energy sources, power grids, and smart building technologies into modern infrastructure.

Qualifications:

Degree in Electrical Engineering (BEng or MEng) – Required for professional recognition.
Institution of Engineering and Technology (IET) Membership – Recognised for career progression.
Chartered Engineer (CEng) or Incorporated Engineer (IEng) Status – Achieved through IET accreditation.
NVQ Level 4, 5, or 6 in Electrical Engineering (for those without a degree) – Alternative pathway.
18th Edition Wiring Regulations (BS 7671) – Mandatory for compliance with UK electrical safety standards.
High Voltage (HV) Training – Required for working with power transmission systems.

Typical Day:

Designing electrical distribution systems, power grids, and circuit layouts.Using
CAD software to create electrical schematics.
Conducting load calculations and energy efficiency assessments.
Inspecting and troubleshooting electrical systems to ensure compliance.
Working on renewable energy projects, integrating solar panels, battery storage, and EV charging stations.
Liaising with construction managers, architects, and mechanical engineers to coordinate installations

Inspector (Building/Site Inspector)

Inspectors ensure that construction meets safety, quality, and legal requirements.

Qualifications:

Degree in Building Surveying or Construction Management.
CIOB or RICS Accreditation.

Typical Day:

Conducting on-site inspections.
Reporting safety violations.

Career Path:

Compliance Officer → Senior Building Inspector.

Designer (General)

Designers in construction play a crucial role in developing concepts, plans, and technical drawings for buildings, infrastructure, and interior spaces. They ensure that projects are not only functional but also meet aesthetic, environmental, and regulatory standards.

Designers often work closely with architects, engineers, and project managers to translate ideas into detailed blueprints used during construction.

Qualifications:

Degree in Design, Architectural Technology, or Civil Engineering – Provides the technical foundation for design roles.
HND/HNC in Construction and the Built Environment – Alternative pathway for those who prefer a vocational route.
BIM (Building Information Modelling) Certification – Essential for working on digital design projects.

AutoCAD/Revit Training – Required for creating and modifying technical drawings.
CIAT (Chartered Institute of Architectural Technologists) Membership – Recognised for career progression in architectural design.

Typical Day:

Developing initial concept sketches and digital models based on client specifications.
Using AutoCAD, Revit, and BIM software to create detailed construction drawings.
Ensuring designs comply with UK building regulations, sustainability standards, and safety codes.
Collaborating with architects, engineers, and site managers to refine technical details.
Revising plans based on client feedback, site conditions, and regulatory requirements.
Conducting site visits to ensure that construction aligns with approved designs.

Career Path:

Junior Designer → Design Coordinator → Senior Designer → Lead Designer → Design Director.
Specialise in residential, commercial, industrial, or sustainable design.
Transition into architectural technology, interior design, or urban planning.
Work as a freelance designer or establish a design consultancy.

Rail Construction: Specialised Roles and Certifications

Rail construction is a highly specialised sector within the construction industry, requiring strict safety standards, technical expertise, and specialised certifications. Workers in this field are responsible for building, maintaining, and upgrading railway infrastructure, ensuring the safe and efficient operation of the rail network.

Due to the high-risk nature of rail work, individuals must obtain specific certifications and competencies before being allowed to work on or near railway tracks.

Below are some of the key roles in rail construction, along with their required qualifications, responsibilities, and career progression opportunities.

Railway Engineer

Railway engineers are responsible for designing, constructing, and maintaining railway tracks, bridges, tunnels, and station infrastructure. They work to ensure that the railway system is safe, efficient, and capable of handling passenger and freight transport needs.

Qualifications:

Degree in Civil Engineering, Railway Engineering, or Mechanical Engineering – Required for professional engineering roles.
Institution of Civil Engineers (ICE) Membership – Recognised for career progression in infrastructure engineering.

Railway Safety and Track Engineering Courses – Provided by industry-recognised training bodies.
Sentinel Card – Mandatory for working on the railway network.
PTS (Personal Track Safety) Certification – Essential for working near live railway tracks.

Typical Day:

Designing track layouts, signalling systems, and supporting infrastructure.
Conducting track inspections and assessing structural integrity.
Supervising railway maintenance and construction activities.
Ensuring compliance with Network Rail safety standards and regulations.

Collaborating with surveyors, project managers, and signalling teams.

Career Path:

Graduate Engineer → Rail Engineer → Senior Rail Engineer → Rail Project Manager → Director of Rail Infrastructure.
Specialise in track maintenance, rail signalling, or high-speed rail projects.
Move into consulting, project management, or transport planning.

Track Operative (Rail Labourer)

Track operatives work on-site, assisting in the installation, maintenance, and repair of railway tracks and associated infrastructure. They perform manual labour and work in teams to ensure railway lines remain safe and functional.

Qualifications:

PTS (Personal Track Safety) Certification – Required for working on or near railway tracks.
Sentinel Card – Issued after completing rail-specific safety training.
Track Induction Course – Provides basic knowledge of track components and maintenance.
Manual Handling and Small Tools Certification – Required for using specialist rail tools.

Typical Day:

Assisting with track installation, realignment, and maintenance.
Inspecting and replacing sleepers, ballast, and rails.
Using specialist railway tools to cut, weld, and fit track components.
Ensuring compliance with health and safety regulations on-site.
Working under the supervision of a Controller of Site Safety (COSS).

Career Path:

Track Operative → Lead Track Operative → Supervisor → Track Engineer.
Specialise in track welding, overhead line equipment (OLE), or signal maintenance.
Progress into site management or railway project coordination.

Controller of Site Safety (COSS)

The Controller of Site Safety (COSS) is responsible for ensuring the safety of workers on railway sites. They supervise work teams and implement safety protocols to prevent accidents near live railway tracks.

Qualifications:

PTS (Personal Track Safety) Certification – Required before training as a COSS.
COSS Training Course – Covers safety responsibilities, risk assessments, and site control.
Sentinel Card – Proof of competency for working in rail environments.
Emergency First Aid at Work Certificate – Recommended for dealing with on-site incidents.

Typical Day:

Conducting site safety briefings before work begins.
Ensuring all workers follow track safety rules and procedures.
Monitoring railway signals and track conditions to prevent hazards.
Liaising with signallers, engineers, and project managers to coordinate safe working practices.

Career Path:

Track Operative → COSS → Rail Safety Supervisor → Rail Site Manager.
Progress into rail project management, health and safety, or compliance auditing.

Signalling Engineer

Signalling engineers design, install, and maintain railway signalling systems that control train movements and ensure safe operations.

Qualifications:

Degree in Electrical, Electronic, or Railway Engineering – Required for professional roles.
IRSE (Institution of Railway Signal Engineers) Membership – Recognised for career development in rail signalling.
PTS (Personal Track Safety) Certification – Mandatory for working near railway tracks.
Sentinel Card – Required for all rail industry professionals.

Typical Day:

Designing signalling layouts and control systems.
Installing and testing railway signal equipment.
Diagnosing and repairing signal faults and failures.
Ensuring compliance with Network Rail safety standards.

Career Path:

Graduate Signalling Engineer → Senior Engineer → Principal Engineer → Signalling Project Manager.
Specialise in digital railway signalling, automated control systems, or high-speed rail networks.

Rail Designer

Rail designers work on the planning, layout, and aesthetics of railway stations, track alignments, and associated infrastructure.

Qualifications:

Degree in Architectural Technology, Civil Engineering, or Transport Design.
BIM (Building Information Modelling) Certification – Essential for digital rail design.
AutoCAD & Revit Training – Required for technical drawings.
PTS (Personal Track Safety) Certification – Required for site visits.

Typical Day:

Creating technical drawings and 3D models for railway infrastructure.
Ensuring compliance with transport regulations and accessibility standards.
Coordinating with engineers and project managers.
Conducting site visits to assess feasibility and project progress.

Career Path:

Junior Rail Designer → Senior Designer → Lead Designer → Rail Project
Coordinator.Specialise in station planning, track alignment design, or urban rail projects.

Highway Construction: Specialised Roles and Certifications

Highway construction is a critical part of the transportation infrastructure, ensuring roads, bridges, and motorways are safe, durable, and capable of handling increasing traffic demands. Professionals in this field are responsible for road design, resurfacing, traffic control, and maintenance. Due to the high-risk environment, specialised training and certifications are required for working on live carriageways.

Below are key roles in highway construction, along with their required qualifications, responsibilities, and career progression opportunities.

Highways Engineer

Highways engineers design and oversee the construction and maintenance of roads, motorways, and drainage systems. They ensure that roads are built to high safety standards, withstand environmental conditions, and accommodate growing traffic needs.

Qualifications:

Degree in Civil Engineering, Highway Engineering, or Transportation Engineering.
Institution of Civil Engineers (ICE) Membership – Recognised for career advancement.
NVQ Level 6 or 7 in Highway Engineering – For experienced professionals without a degree.

Road Safety Audit Training – Essential for engineers involved in safety assessments.

Typical Day:

Designing road layouts, drainage systems, and traffic flow models.
Supervising road construction and resurfacing projects.
Conducting safety audits and traffic impact assessments.
Ensuring compliance with Highways England and local authority regulations.
Coordinating with surveyors, traffic planners, and site managers.

Career Path:

Graduate Engineer → Highways Engineer → Senior Engineer → Principal Engineer → Director of Highways Projects.
Specialise in intelligent transport systems, sustainable road design, or major motorway projects.
Move into consulting, government transport planning, or project management.

Road Surfacing Operative

Road surfacing operatives lay and repair asphalt, concrete, and other road surfaces. They ensure highways are smooth, durable, and resistant to wear and weather conditions.

Qualifications:

NVQ Level 2 in Road Surfacing.
CSCS (Construction Skills Certification Scheme) Card – Required for working on highways.

NPORS (National Plant Operators Registration Scheme) or CPCS (Construction Plant Competence Scheme) – Required for operating road surfacing machinery.
Health and Safety in Road Work Training – Covers manual handling and safety procedures.

Typical Day:

Operating asphalt pavers, compactors, and road rollers.
Spreading and levelling tarmac, concrete, and other road surfacing materials.
Repairing potholes, cracks, and uneven surfaces.
Working alongside highway engineers and traffic management teams.

Career Path:

Surfacing Operative → Lead Operative → Site Supervisor → Surfacing Project Manager.
Specialise in machine operation, road marking, or pavement engineering.

Traffic Management Operative (TM Operative)

Traffic management operatives are responsible for controlling and directing traffic around roadworks, ensuring the safety of both workers and the public.

Qualifications:

LANTRA NHSS 12AB or 12D Training – National Highways Sector Scheme accreditation for traffic management.
CSCS Card – Required for general highway work.

First Aid Training – Recommended for emergency response on-site.

Typical Day:

Setting up temporary traffic lights, cones, and lane closures.
Directing traffic and pedestrians safely around work zones.
Communicating with site supervisors and highway maintenance teams.
Ensuring compliance with Highways England road safety regulations.

Career Path:

TM Operative → Lead Traffic Controller → Traffic Manager → Highway Safety Coordinator.
Specialise in motorway traffic control, emergency response, or road signage planning.

Bridge Inspector

Bridge inspectors assess the structural integrity of bridges and overpasses, ensuring they are safe and compliant with engineering standards.

Qualifications:

Degree in Civil Engineering or Structural Engineering.
NVQ Level 6 in Structural Inspection – For professionals without a degree.
IRATA (Industrial Rope Access Trade Association) Certification – Required for rope access bridge inspections.

PASMA (Prefabricated Access Suppliers' and Manufacturers' Association) Training – For working on scaffolding and temporary access structures.

Typical Day:

Conducting visual and technical inspections of bridges and flyovers.
Using drones, sensors, and 3D scanning equipment to assess bridge conditions.
Identifying cracks, corrosion, and structural weaknesses.
Producing inspection reports and recommending maintenance strategies.

Career Path:

Bridge Inspector → Senior Inspector → Structural Engineer → Director of Bridge Safety.
Specialise in historic bridge restoration, earthquake-resistant design, or advanced inspection technologies.

Highway Designer

Highway designers create road layouts, traffic flow models, and urban transport plans to improve safety and efficiency.

Qualifications:

Degree in Transport Design, Civil Engineering, or Architectural Technology.
BIM (Building Information Modelling) Certification – Required for digital infrastructure design.
AutoCAD & Revit Training – Essential for technical drawings and 3D modelling.

Typical Day:

Designing road intersections, roundabouts, and lane configurations.
Ensuring compliance with Department for Transport (DfT) guidelines.
Coordinating with highways engineers and local authorities.Conducting environmental impact assessments for new road projects.

Career Path:

Junior Designer → Senior Designer → Lead Designer → Transport Planning Manager.
Specialise in sustainable highway design, urban mobility, or smart road systems.

Other Specialised Roles in Construction

Beyond the core roles in skilled trades, engineering, project management, rail, and highway construction, there are several highly specialised roles that contribute to the safety, efficiency, and functionality of modern buildings and infrastructure. These roles require specific training, technical expertise, and industry-recognized certifications.

Below is a summary of some of these specialised careers.

Fire Systems Installer / Fire Engineer

Fire safety professionals design, install, and maintain fire detection and suppression systems in buildings.

Fire systems installers focus on alarm systems, sprinklers, and emergency exits, while fire engineers work on fire risk assessments, safety compliance, and advanced fire suppression technologies.

Qualifications: NVQ Level 2 or 3 in Fire Detection and Alarm Systems,
FIA (Fire Industry Association) Certification,
IFE (Institution of Fire Engineers) Membership.

Career Path: Fire Systems Technician → Lead Installer → Fire Safety Consultant → Fire Engineer.

Telecommunication Installer / Engineer

Telecommunication professionals install and maintain network infrastructure, fibre optic cabling, and wireless communication systems for buildings and large-scale developments. They ensure that sites have reliable internet, telephone, and security communication systems.

Qualifications: NVQ Level 2 or 3 in Telecommunications,
Fibre Optic Installation Certification,
ECS (Electrotechnical Certification Scheme) Card.

Career Path: Installer → Network Engineer → Lead Telecommunications Engineer → Systems Integration Specialist.

Lift / Elevator Installer and Engineer

These specialists install, repair, and maintain lifts, escalators, and automated vertical transport systems in commercial and residential buildings.

Qualifications: NVQ Level 3 in Lift and Escalator Engineering, LEIA (Lift & Escalator Industry Association) Certification, CSCS Card.

Career Path: Lift Technician → Senior Engineer → Lift System Designer → Vertical Transport Consultant.

Building Automation & Smart Systems Technician

Technicians in this field work on smart building systems, home automation, and energy-efficient technologies, integrating automated lighting, heating, and security systems.

Qualifications: NVQ Level 3 in Building Controls,
KNX (Smart Building Systems) Certification,
BMS (Building Management Systems) Training.

Career Path: Technician → Systems Engineer → BMS Specialist → Smart Infrastructure Consultant.

Geotechnical Technician

Geotechnical specialists assess soil conditions, ground stability, and environmental factors before construction begins, ensuring safe foundation designs.

Qualifications: Degree in Geotechnical Engineering,
NVQ Level 3 in Site Investigation,
ICE Membership.

Career Path: Field Technician → Geotechnical Engineer → Senior Geotechnical Consultant.

Environmental Engineer / Sustainability Consultant

Selected Roles & Positions in the Construction Industry

- **Skilled Trades**
  - Painter and Decorator
  - Electricians
  - Plumber
  - Carpenter and Joiner
  - Plasterer
  - Bricklayer
  - Machine Operator
- **Professional Roles: Managing and Planning Construction Projects**
  - Architect
  - Quantity Surveyor
  - Project Manager
  - Construction Manager
  - Site Supervisor
- **Engineering and Design Roles in Construction**
  - Civil Engineer
  - Structural Engineer
  - Mechanical Engineer
  - Electrical Engineer
  - Inspector (Building/Site Inspector)
  - Designer (General)
- **Rail Construction: Specialised Roles and Certifications**
  - Railway Engineer
  - Track Operative (Rail Labourer)
  - Controller of Site Safety (COSS)
  - Signalling Engineer
  - Rail Designer
- **Highway Construction: Specialised Roles and Certifications**
  - Highways Engineer
  - Road Surfacing Operative
  - Traffic Management Operative (TM Operative)
  - Bridge Inspector
- **Other Specialised Roles in Construction**
  - Fire Systems Installer / Fire Engineer
  - Telecommunication Installer / Engineer
  - Lift / Elevator Installer and Engineer
  - Building Automation & Smart Systems Technician
  - Geotechnical Technician

Final Thoughts

The construction industry offers a diverse range of career paths, from hands-on skilled trades to specialized engineering and design roles, as well as management positions in highways, rail, and general construction projects. Each role plays a vital part in ensuring that buildings, infrastructure, and transport networks are safe, efficient, and sustainable.

Skilled tradespeople such as electricians, plumbers, and carpenters bring construction projects to life, working on the ground to create the structures we rely on every day. Professional roles, including architects, engineers, and quantity surveyors, focus on the planning, design, and cost management of projects, ensuring they meet industry standards and client expectations.

Rail and highway construction specialists work in high-risk environments, requiring additional safety training and certifications to keep transport systems running efficiently.

These careers demand technical expertise, leadership skills, and continuous learning. By obtaining the right qualifications and industry-recognised certifications, individuals can progress from entry-level positions to senior management, consultancy, or even establish their own firms. As the industry continues to evolve with advancements in technology, sustainability, and infrastructure development, opportunities for career growth will only expand.

No matter your background or skill set, construction offers exciting, rewarding, and long-term career prospects. Choosing the right path and committing to professional development can open doors to a successful and fulfilling future in the industry.

6. Gaining Skills and Qualifications

Success in the construction sector requires not only practical experience but also the acquisition of the necessary skills and qualifications. With the right training, you can move up in your position and get better pay and more specialised roles.

In this chapter, we'll look at the required qualifications, the value of soft skills, health and safety training, and the benefits of specialisation.

Essential Construction Qualifications

The construction skills you need depend on the job you want. These certifications are essential for demonstrating your abilities and meeting industry standards:

NVQs (National Vocational Qualifications):

NVQs are practical, work-based qualifications that are highly regarded in the industry.

Common NVQs include:

Level 2: Suitable for entry-level trades like bricklaying, carpentry, and plumbing.

Level 3: Aimed at those looking to specialise further or take on supervisory responsibilities.

Level 4-7: Designed for management-level roles, such as site managers or construction project managers.

NVQs are assessed on-site by evaluating your competence in real-world scenarios.

City & Guilds Diplomas:

Widely recognised qualifications offering structured learning for trades like electrical installation, welding, and plumbing.

Often a first step before progressing to NVQs or more advanced certifications.

HNDs (Higher National Diplomas) and Foundation Degrees:

Ideal for roles that require technical knowledge, such as civil engineering, quantity surveying, or construction management.

HNDs combine academic learning with practical skills, bridging the gap between vocational and university-level education.

For those entering specialised areas, such as rail construction, additional qualifications like the Sentinel Card and Personal Track Safety (PTS) certification are required.

The Importance of Soft Skills

Technical certifications are essential, but soft skills are just as crucial in the construction profession. Companies highly prize effective communicators, team players, and challenge-adaptable professionals.

Key soft skills include:

Communication: Clear communication ensures that instructions are followed, problems are resolved, and projects run smoothly.

Teamwork: Construction projects rely on the collective effort of a team. Being able to work collaboratively with others is essential.

Problem-Solving: Unexpected challenges are common on construction sites. The ability to think critically and propose solutions is highly valued.

Time Management: Construction work is deadline-driven. Being able to manage your time effectively ensures projects are completed on schedule.

Investing in these skills can set you apart from others in the industry and prepare for leadership roles.

Training in Health and Safety Regulations

The construction sector revolves mainly around safety. Good training guarantees your own safety and the safety of every other person on-site.

CITB Health and Safety Training:

The Construction Industry Training Board (CITB) offers a range of safety courses, including:

Site Safety Plus: Covers basic health and safety practices for workers and supervisors.

SSSTS (Site Supervisor Safety Training Scheme): Aimed at those overseeing teams on-site.

SMSTS (Site Management Safety Training Scheme): For site managers responsible for enforcing safety procedures.

CSCS (Construction Skills Certification Scheme):

Most construction sites in the UK require workers to hold a CSCS card. Obtaining the card involves passing a Health, Safety, and Environment Test.

First Aid Training:

Many employers value workers trained in first aid, which can be critical in responding to on-site emergencies.

Investing in health and safety training not only makes you a safer worker but also increases your employability.

Specialising in Skills: Stand Out in the Industry.

Specialising in a particular area of construction can boost your career prospects and earning potential.

Sustainable Building:

The demand for eco-friendly construction is growing. Training in sustainable building techniques, such as using energy-efficient materials or renewable energy systems, can set you apart in this emerging field.

Relevant certifications include BREEAM (Building Research Establishment Environmental Assessment Method) and LEED (Leadership in Energy and Environmental Design).

Technology in Construction:

Technology is transforming the construction industry. Specialising in areas like Building Information Modelling (BIM) or using drones for site surveys can give you a competitive edge.

Courses and certifications in BIM, 3D modelling, or digital construction tools are becoming increasingly valuable.

Testing and Inspection:

Specialising in electrical testing and commissioning, or portable appliance testing (PAT), can open up niche roles within the industry.

Specialisation allows you to carve out a unique career path and position yourself as an expert in your field.

Final Thoughts

To have a successful job in construction, you need the right skills and credentials. From practical NVQs to advanced certificates in sustainability and technology, your training will enhance your skills and increase your professional value.

In the following chapter, we'll discuss the pros and cons of working in construction. This will help you get ready for both the good and bad sides of this fast-paced field.

7. Advantages and Drawbacks of Working in Construction

There are many chances to grow personally and professionally in the construction business, but as with any job, there are also some challenges. This chapter will talk about the main pros and cons of working in construction and ways to deal with these challenges so you can do well in your job.

Advantages of a Career in Construction

A career in construction offers many benefits, making it a popular choice for those who enjoy hands-on work and building a tangible legacy.

Competitive Pay:

Construction offers a range of well-paying roles, even at entry level. For example, skilled trades like electricians and plumbers often earn salaries above the national average, with potential for further income through overtime or self-employment.

As you gain experience and qualifications, your earning potential increases significantly.

Job Satisfaction:

Few industries provide the same sense of accomplishment as construction. The ability to see the results of your work—whether it's a new building, a road, or a piece of infrastructure—creates a lasting sense of pride.

Working in construction allows you to make a tangible impact on communities, improving the spaces where people live, work, and travel.

Career Progression:

The construction industry offers clear pathways for advancement. Whether you start as an apprentice or in an entry-level role, you can work your way up to supervisory or management positions.

Opportunities for specialisation, such as sustainable building or advanced construction technology, provide additional avenues for growth.

Variety of Work:

No two days in construction are the same. Whether you're working on different projects, learning new techniques, or collaborating with diverse teams, the industry keeps things interesting and dynamic.

Stability and Demand:

The construction sector remains a cornerstone of the UK economy, with ongoing demand for skilled workers. Major infrastructure projects, housing developments, and green energy initiatives mean there's no shortage of work for those with the right skills.

Drawbacks of Working in Construction

While the construction industry offers numerous advantages, it's important to be aware of the challenges you might face.

Physical Demands:

Many construction roles require physical strength and endurance. Long hours of lifting, bending, and standing can take a toll on your body over time.

Working outdoors means you're exposed to weather conditions, whether it's scorching heat in summer or freezing cold in winter.

Demanding Schedules:

Construction work often involves tight deadlines. Some projects require early mornings, late nights, or weekend work to meet completion goals.

If you're working in a project-based role, there may be periods of downtime between jobs, especially in self-employment.

Safety Risks:

Construction sites can be hazardous environments. Accidents involving heavy machinery, falls, or exposure to harmful substances are potential risks.

Strict adherence to safety protocols is essential, but the risks can still create stress for some workers.

Work-Life Balance:

For those in demanding roles, especially management or self-employment, maintaining a healthy work-life balance can be challenging. Long hours and travel may impact personal time.

Strategies to Overcome Challenges

The challenges of construction don't have to stand in the way of a rewarding career. By adopting the right mindset and strategies, you can navigate these difficulties effectively.

Maintain Your Physical Health:

Regular exercise, proper lifting techniques, and stretching can help you avoid injuries and build stamina.

Ensure you have the correct PPE (personal protective equipment) to protect against workplace hazards.

Prioritise Safety:

Attend regular safety training to stay updated on best practices.

Report hazards immediately and never take shortcuts when it comes to safety.

Manage Your Time Effectively:

Use scheduling tools and apps to plan your workload and avoid burnout.

Set boundaries to ensure you have time for rest and personal commitments.

Focus on Professional Development:

Gaining additional qualifications, such as advanced health and safety certifications, can help you progress to less physically demanding roles.

Specialising in fields like design, planning, or sustainability can open doors to office-based or leadership positions.

Build a Support Network:

Strong relationships with colleagues and mentors can provide support during challenging times.

Joining trade unions or professional organisations can connect you with resources to help manage workplace issues.

Strategies to Overcome Challenges

- Maintain Your Physical Health:
- Prioritize Safety
- Manage Your Time Effectively
- Focus on Professional Development
- Build a Support Network

Final Thoughts

Although building work can be demanding, tangible and intangible benefits make the effort worthwhile. By seeing possible challenges and taking proactive actions to address them, you can have a long and rewarding career in the sector.

In the following chapter, we'll look at how to prepare for long-term success in construction, including career advancement, skill diversification, and transferring into management or self-employment.

8. Planning for Long-Term Success

Construction offers a wealth of opportunities for growth and advancement. Whether you aspire to move into management, start your own business, or specialise in cutting-edge technologies, the industry provides numerous pathways to achieve your goals.

This chapter will guide you through building a sustainable and successful career in construction by exploring growth opportunities, skill diversification, and staying ahead of industry trends.

Building a Career Ladder in Construction

Advancement in construction is often determined by a combination of experience, qualifications, and a proactive commitment to career growth.

Start with a Strong Foundation:

Begin your career with hands-on roles or apprenticeships to gain practical experience.

Complete essential qualifications such as NVQs or industry-specific certifications.

Set Career Goals:

Outline short-term and long-term goals, such as progressing to a supervisor or management position.

Regularly evaluate your progress and adjust your goals based on your experiences and interests.

Gain Relevant Experience:

Seek opportunities to work on diverse projects, which will expose you to new challenges and techniques.

Volunteer for leadership responsibilities, such as supervising small teams or coordinating tasks, to build management experience.

Pursue Advanced Qualifications:

Invest in higher-level certifications, such as NVQ Level 4 in Construction Site Supervision or Level 6 in Construction Site Management.

Consider academic pathways, such as HNDs or degrees in construction management or civil engineering, for senior roles.

Building a career ladder in construction is about taking incremental steps, being open to learning, and staying focused on your long-term goals.

Diversify Your Skills to Increase Career Flexibility

Diversifying your skill set can open up new opportunities and increase your resilience in the face of industry changes.

Explore Additional Trades:

If you're already skilled in one area, consider learning complementary trades. For example, an electrician might benefit from learning about renewable energy systems like solar panel installation.

Short courses or part-time training programs can help you gain new certifications while continuing to work.

Develop Soft Skills:

Skills like communication, problem-solving, and negotiation are critical for roles in leadership, project management, or client-facing positions.

Attend workshops or enrol in online courses to enhance these skills.

Specialise in In-Demand Areas:

Consider specialising in areas like green construction, advanced machinery operation, or digital technologies like Building Information Modelling (BIM).

Specialized skills not only make you more marketable but often come with higher pay and greater job security.

Diversification helps you adapt to shifts in the construction industry and keeps your career dynamic and fulfilling.

Pathways to Supervisory, Management, or Self-Employment Roles

As you gain experience and qualifications, you may wish to move into leadership roles or explore self-employment opportunities.

Supervisory and Management Roles:

Start by taking on smaller leadership tasks, such as supervising a team or coordinating site logistics.

Complete certifications like the SSSTS (Site Supervisor Safety Training Scheme) or SMSTS (Site Management Safety Training Scheme) to qualify for these roles.

Management roles often require strong organisational and communication skills, so focus on developing these early in your career.

Self-Employment:

Many skilled tradespeople, such as electricians, plumbers, and builders, choose self-employment for its flexibility and earning potential.

To succeed as a self-employed professional:

Build a strong reputation through quality work and excellent customer service.
Obtain the necessary business licenses and insurance.
Learn basic business skills, such as budgeting, marketing, and client management.

Platforms like Checkatrade or Rated People can help you find work as a self-employed tradesperson.

Senior Roles in Project Management:

For those interested in overseeing entire projects, roles like project manager or contracts manager offer the opportunity to lead teams and ensure projects are delivered on time and within budget.

Consider advanced qualifications like a PRINCE2 certification or a degree in construction management.
Whether you aim to lead teams or run your own business, planning your path carefully will help you achieve your ambitions.

Staying Updated with Industry Trends

The construction business is rapidly changing, and new technology, processes, and expectations are impacting how projects are executed. Keeping up with these trends might set you apart as a forward-thinking professional.

Embrace Technology:

Tools like drones, 3D printing, and augmented reality are becoming increasingly common on construction sites. Learning to use these technologies can set you apart.

Building Information Modelling (BIM) is revolutionising project planning and management—gaining BIM certification can significantly boost your career prospects.

Focus on Sustainability:

Green construction and energy-efficient building techniques are in high demand as the industry moves toward net-zero goals.
Certifications like BREEAM or courses in renewable energy installation can help you stay competitive in this growing sector.

Participate in Professional Development:

Attend trade shows, conferences, and workshops to stay updated on the latest innovations.
Join industry organisations or unions to network and access exclusive training opportunities.
Adapting to industry changes ensures you remain valuable to employers and clients, no matter how the construction landscape evolves.

Final Thoughts

For long-term success in construction, you need to do more than work hard. You also need to set clear goals, learn new skills, and keep up with changes in the industry. Getting a rewarding job that grows with the business is possible if you know what to do.

In the next chapter, we'll guide you through additional resources and practical tools to help you continue building your future in construction.

9. Resources and Where to Go From Here

Having the right tools can make all the difference as you start your job in construction. In this part, you'll find a carefully chosen collection of websites, groups, and tools that can help you find work, learn more, and stay supported as you go. You'll also find a helpful checklist to help you get started in your new career.

Top Websites for Job Hunting in the Construction Industry

The construction industry in the UK offers a range of platforms dedicated to connecting job seekers with employers. These websites are ideal for finding entry-level roles, apprenticeships, and skilled positions:

Indeed (*www.indeed.co.uk*): A comprehensive job search engine with thousands of construction-related job listings.

Totaljobs (*www.totaljobs.com*): Features a wide variety of construction roles, from labourers to project managers.

CITB Apprenticeships (*www.citb.co.uk*): The go-to resource for finding apprenticeships and training opportunities.

Gov.uk Find an Apprenticeship (*https://www.gov.uk/apply-apprenticeship*): A government-backed platform for locating apprenticeship programs across the UK.

Construction Enquirer Jobs (*www.constructionenquirer.com*): A specialised site focused on construction industry roles.

Checkatrade (*www.checkatrade.com*): Ideal for those looking to start as self-employed tradespeople or find subcontracting opportunities.

Linkedin (*www.linkedin.com*): The platform used for professional networking and career development.

Spending time on these platforms can help you identify job opportunities that align with your skills and interests.

Further Reading and Professional Development Resources

Staying informed and continuously learning are key to advancing in construction.

Here are some recommended resources to deepen your knowledge:

Books:

"Modern Construction Handbook" by Andrew Watts – A comprehensive guide to modern construction techniques and materials.

"The Construction Management Handbook" by David Langford – Ideal for those pursuing leadership roles in the industry.

Online Learning Platforms:

FutureLearn (*www.futurelearn.com*): Offers free and paid courses in construction management, sustainability, and more.

Udemy (*www.udemy.com*): Features affordable courses on technical skills, including Building Information Modelling (BIM) and project management.

Industry Publications:

Construction News (*www.constructionnews.co.uk*): Stay updated with the latest industry trends, projects, and developments.

The Builders Merchant Journal (*www.buildersmerchantsnews.co.uk*): A valuable resource for trade-specific news and insights.

Regularly engaging with these resources can help you stay ahead in a competitive and ever-evolving industry.

Useful Organisations and Unions

The construction industry has several organisations and unions dedicated to supporting workers and advancing the sector. Here are some key ones to know:

CITB (Construction Industry Training Board):

Provides training, grants, and funding for apprenticeships. Website: *www.citb.co.uk*

FMB (Federation of Master Builders):

Supports small and medium-sized construction firms with resources, advice, and networking opportunities.
Website: *www.fmb.org.uk*

Unite the Union:

Represents workers across various trades, offering legal advice, workplace support, and campaigning for better conditions.
Website: *www.unitetheunion.org*

The Chartered Institute of Building (CIOB):

Promotes professional standards in construction and offers memberships, training, and certifications.
Website: *www.ciob.org*

The Royal Institution of Chartered Surveyors (RICS):

Supports those in surveying and related professions with training, networking, and accreditation.
Website: *www.rics.org*

Joining these organisations can provide valuable resources, training, and a sense of community within the industry.

Checklist to Kickstart Your Construction Career

Here's a step-by-step checklist to guide you as you start your journey:

☑ **Research Roles:**

Explore different roles in construction and identify the ones that align with your interests and strengths.

☑ **Obtain Essential Certifications:**

Apply for your CSCS card and complete any necessary health and safety training.
For rail work, ensure you acquire a Sentinel Card and PTS certification.

☑ **Update Your CV:**

Tailor your CV to construction roles, highlighting relevant skills, experience, and certifications.

☑ **Start Networking:**

Attend job fairs, trade shows, and connect with professionals on LinkedIn.

☑ **Apply for Jobs:**

Search job boards and company websites for apprenticeships, traineeships, or entry-level positions.

☑ **Continue Learning:**

Enrol in courses to develop additional skills, such as sustainability practices, BIM, or advanced health and safety certifications.

☑ **Build a Support Network:**

Join professional organisations and unions to access resources and connect with peers in the industry.

☑ **Set Career Goals:**

Outline short-term and long-term objectives, such as advancing to supervisory roles or specialising in a trade.

Checklist to Kickstart Your Construction Career

- [ ] Obtain Essential Certifications:
- [ ] Update Your CV
- [ ] Start Networking & Build a Support Network
- [ ] Apply for Jobs
- [ ] Continue Learning
- [ ] Set Career Goals

Final Thoughts

Starting a career in construction is a fantastic approach for taking a road full of possibilities for both professional and personal development.

With the information, tools, and resources in this chapter, you'll be ready to take your first steps with confidence and build a long-lasting job in the field.

In the next chapter, we'll explore how to manage in construction when you are not a native English speaker.

10. Navigating Construction Work as a Non-Native English Speaker

The UK construction sector employs a varied workforce from nations including Poland, Romania, Italy, India, and many others. You don't have to speak English perfectly to do well in construction, but it is important to be able to communicate clearly for safety, teamwork, and job advancement.

This chapter gives useful tips and advice to help you do well in the UK construction industry, even if English isn't your first language. It also gives you guidance on knowing your rights and seeking workplace support.

The Importance of Communication in Construction

Construction sites are fast-paced environments where clear communication is crucial for:

Following safety procedures to prevent accidents and injuries.
Understanding instructions from supervisors, site managers, or colleagues.
Collaborating with teams on tasks, ensuring work is done correctly.
Reporting hazards or issues that could impact safety or project quality.
Reading construction drawings, labels, and safety signs to avoid mistakes.
Even if you are skilled in your trade, misunderstandings due to language barriers can create risks for you and your colleagues.

Practical Tips to Overcome Language Barriers

Learn Key Construction Vocabulary

Focus on the most commonly used words and phrases in construction (see vocabulary list below).
Use flashcards or mobile apps like Duolingo, Anki, or Quizlet to memorise new words.
Label tools and equipment in English in your workplace or home to reinforce learning.
Improve Listening and Speaking SkillsListen carefully to supervisors and colleagues.
If unsure, repeat instructions back to confirm understanding.
Watch construction-related videos on YouTube to hear industry-specific English in use.
Practice speaking with colleagues or attend local English conversation groups.
Use Translation and Communication ToolsGoogle Translate: Quickly translate words and phrases.
SayHi or iTranslate apps: Help with spoken communication.
Linguee: Provides example sentences for technical construction terms.
Ask for Clarification

If you don't understand an instruction, ask politely:

⊡ Avoid: "I don't understand."

✓ Say: "Could you please explain that again?" or "Can you show me what you mean?"

Use visual cues—pointing at materials or equipment can help clarify meaning.

Take Advantage of Workplace Support

Many construction companies provide language support or training programs—ask your employer if they offer assistance. Join a union or worker support group (e.g., Unite the Union, GMB, or UCATT) for guidance on rights, training, and workplace issues.

Practical Tips to Overcome Language Barriers

- Learn key construction vocabulary
- Understand construction safety terms to stay compliant on-site.
- Use translation and communication tools
- Take advantage of free learning resources to boost your English skills.
- Ask for Clarification
  - Avoid: "I don't understand.
  - Say: "Could you please explain that again?"
- Take advantage of workplace Support and free learning resources

Understanding Your Workplace Rights

As a non-native English speaker working in the UK construction industry, you have the same legal rights as any other worker.

Right to a Safe Workplace

Your employer must provide safety training in a way that you can understand.
You have the right to refuse unsafe work—if you don't understand an instruction and it seems dangerous, ask for clarification.

Right to Fair Pay and Working Hours

You must be paid at least the UK minimum wage or higher, depending on your contract.
Your payslip should be in a language you can understand—ask for help if needed.

Right to Join a Union

Unions like Unite, GMB, and UCATT support workers in case of disputes, workplace mistreatment, or unfair pay.

Right to Report Discrimination

Employers cannot discriminate based on language, nationality, or background.
If you feel mistreated, seek help from your HR department, a union, or ACAS (Advisory, Conciliation and Arbitration Service).

Additional Learning Resources

Free ESOL (English for Speakers of Other Languages) Classes – Many local councils offer free or low-cost English courses. Visit *www.gov.uk/english-language-classes* to find courses near you.

BBC Learning English – Free online courses and workplace English lessons: *www.bbc.co.uk/learningenglish*.

FutureLearn – Offers construction-specific English courses: *www.futurelearn.com*.

Final Thoughts

Working in construction as a non-native English speaker can be difficult, but the language should never prevent you from success.

You can be more confident, safe, and productive on any construction job if you know your rights, learn new words, and talk to people better.

As you keep practising and get more work experience, your English will get better on its own. This will make it easier to find work in the field. To do well in construction, you need to be able to talk to people well. This is true whether you want to be a project manager, a skilled tradesperson, or a site supervisor.

11. Starting Strong – Practical Advice for Your First Job in Construction

Congratulations—you've secured your first job in construction! Starting strong is key to building a successful career, and this chapter will provide practical advice to help you adapt quickly, stay safe, and thrive in your new role.

From understanding site expectations to setting goals for the future, these tips will set you up for long-term success.

Understanding Site Rules and Expectations

Every construction site operates under strict rules to ensure safety, efficiency, and collaboration. As a newcomer, understanding and adhering to these expectations will help you integrate smoothly into your team.

Punctuality: Arrive on time—or better yet, early—to show your reliability and commitment.

Respect the Chain of Command: Follow instructions from supervisors and team leaders, and address any questions to the appropriate person.

Be Observant: Learn the layout of the site, the location of tools and materials, and the designated safety zones.

Documentation: Always carry your CSCS card or other required certifications, as they may be checked regularly.

Making an effort to understand and follow site rules will demonstrate your professionalism and help you gain the respect of your colleagues.

Prioritise Safety on the Job

Safety is the top priority on any construction site. Even experienced workers rely on proper procedures and equipment to avoid accidents.

Wear Your PPE: Always wear your Personal Protective Equipment, including a hard hat, steel-toe boots, high-visibility clothing, gloves, and goggles, as required.

Stay Alert: Be aware of your surroundings, particularly when working near heavy machinery, vehicles, or elevated areas.

Report Hazards: If you notice unsafe conditions or equipment, report them immediately to your supervisor.

Follow Training: Apply what you've learned in your health and safety courses, such as the correct way to lift heavy materials or use tools safely.

Remember, safety is a shared responsibility. By prioritising your own safety and that of your colleagues, you'll build trust and set a positive example.

Learn from Experienced Colleagues

Your first job is an invaluable opportunity to learn from those around you. Experienced colleagues can offer tips and insights that textbooks and courses might not cover.

Ask Questions: Don't hesitate to seek clarification if you're unsure about a task or procedure. Most seasoned workers are happy to share their knowledge.

Observe Techniques: Pay close attention to how skilled tradespeople carry out their work, from how they use tools to how they solve problems on-site.

Take Notes: Keep a small notebook to jot down techniques, advice, or site procedures you want to remember.

Learning from your colleagues not only enhances your skills but also fosters strong working relationships.

Make a Positive Impression

Your attitude and work ethic will leave a lasting impression on your team and supervisors. By standing out as a reliable and motivated worker, you'll increase your chances of being offered more responsibilities—and opportunities for growth.

Be Proactive: Volunteer for tasks, even if they're outside your immediate role, to show your willingness to contribute.

Stay Professional: Treat everyone on-site with respect, maintain a positive attitude, and communicate clearly.

Take Ownership: If you make a mistake, own up to it and learn from the experience. Supervisors respect workers who take responsibility and strive to improve.

A strong first impression can lead to long-term benefits, including recommendations and offers for more advanced roles.

Take Care of Your Physical Health and Well-Being

Construction work can be physically demanding, so looking after your body and mind is essential for maintaining effectiveness on the job.

Stay Hydrated: Dehydration can affect your concentration and stamina, so drink plenty of water throughout the day.

Eat Well: Fuel your body with nutritious meals and snacks to sustain your energy levels.

Stretch and Rest: Take time to stretch during breaks to prevent strain or injury, and ensure you get adequate rest after a long day.

Manage Stress: Construction work can be challenging, so take steps to relax and recharge outside of work. Hobbies, exercise, or time with family can help you maintain a healthy work-life balance.

Prioritising your well-being will not only improve your performance but also help you avoid burnout.

Set Short-Term and Long-Term Goals

Starting a career in construction is just the beginning. Setting clear goals will help you focus on your growth and take advantage of the opportunities ahead.

Short-Term Goals:

Master the basics of your current role, such as safely using tools and understanding site procedures.

Build a positive relationship with your team and supervisor. Gain any additional certifications required for your role, such as first aid training or specialised equipment licenses.

Long-Term Goals:

Identify roles or trades you'd like to move into, such as becoming a site supervisor or specialising in a particular skill. Work toward advanced qualifications like NVQs or management certifications to prepare for leadership roles. Explore opportunities for self-employment or starting your own business if that aligns with your ambitions.
Tracking your goals and progress can help you stay motivated and ensure your career develops in the direction you want.

Final Thoughts

The first job you get in construction is an important step towards a long and successful career. Knowing what is expected on the job site, putting safety first, learning from others, and taking care of yourself are all things that will help you grow in the future.

You can do anything in this fast-paced business as long as you are proactive and have a clear picture of your goals.

In the next chapter, we'll wrap up the book with some important lessons learnt and some final words of support to help you feel confident as you move forward.

Conclusion

Congratulations on taking the time to explore what a career in construction could mean for you. By now, you've gained a clear understanding of the industry, the pathways to enter it, and how to build a successful, fulfilling career.

The next step is up to you—taking action to turn your ambitions into reality.

The construction industry is about more than just constructing buildings, laying bricks, and installing wiring; it is about creating something long-lasting, something tangible. Few occupations allow you to take a step back at the end of the day and see the real-world impact of your efforts.

Whether it's the first home a family will ever reside in, a towering skyscraper that marks a city skyline, or an industrial facility that powers enterprises, your efforts have a lasting impact on the globe.

There is a great sense of pride in knowing that the roads you help create will connect communities, the bridges you reinforce will transport generations of travellers, and the homes you build will become places of memories.

The sensation of seeing a finished creation that began as an idea and knowing you played a part in making it a reality is extremely remarkable.

Of course, construction presents its own set of challenges. The work can be physically hard, with tight timetables and a steep learning process. There will be early starts, long days, and unexpected challenges to face.

However, the benefits—competitive salary, job satisfaction, professional advancement, and the opportunity to see your work have a real impact—are well worth the effort.

The secret to success is perseverance and a dedication to lifelong learning. Stay curious, learn new skills, and adapt to the changing demands of the market. Whether it's obtaining a new certification, learning a specialised skill, or embracing newer technologies, each step will help you get closer to achieving your goals.

Remember, you don't have to have everything figured out on day one. Start small, make realistic plans, and progress your profession one step at a time. Every milestone, no matter how little, is a step towards your future.

The construction industry wants people like you—motivated, talented, and eager to make a difference. So take the first step. Explore the professions that interest you, network with others in the sector, and start establishing the groundwork for your future.

Your journey into construction begins here. With commitment, hard work, and the appropriate perspective, there is no limit to what you may achieve.

Best of luck and may your career be as powerful and lasting as the structures you help create.

Glossary of Construction Terms

A

Apprenticeship – A structured training program that combines paid work with formal education in a specific trade.

Architect – A professional responsible for designing buildings and ensuring they meet safety, function, and aesthetic requirements.

Asbestos Awareness (Category A Training) – A mandatory health and safety course for workers who may come into contact with asbestos-containing materials.

Appointed Person (Electrical Works) – A competent individual designated to take responsibility for electrical safety on-site. This role involves risk assessments, issuing permits to work, ensuring compliance with BS 7671 Wiring Regulations, and overseeing high-voltage (HV) and low-voltage (LV) electrical operations. The Appointed Person is crucial in preventing electrical hazards and ensuring safe work procedures.

B

Banksman – A site worker responsible for directing vehicle and crane movements, ensuring site safety.

Bricklayer – A skilled tradesperson who builds walls, partitions, and other structures using bricks and mortar.

Building Regulations – A set of standards governing the design, construction, and alteration of buildings in the UK.

BS 7671 (Wiring Regulations) – The UK standard for electrical installations, ensuring safety, design, installation, and testing of electrical systems. Compliance is required for all electrical work.

C

Carpenter & Joiner – A skilled worker specialising in cutting, shaping, and fitting wood for buildings.

CIS (Construction Industry Scheme) – A tax scheme for self-employed construction workers where contractors deduct tax at source before payment.

CITB (Construction Industry Training Board) – The UK's training body for the construction industry, responsible for funding and certification.

CSCS (Construction Skills Certification Scheme) Card – A card proving that a worker has the required health and safety training to work on UK construction sites.

Contractor – A person or company hired to complete a specific construction project or task.

Controller of Site Safety (COSS) – A rail worker responsible for ensuring safety procedures are followed when working on railway tracks.

Construction Manager – A professional overseeing the planning, coordination, and execution of construction projects.

Competent Person – Someone with the training, experience, and knowledge to safely carry out specific construction tasks, as defined by health & safety regulations.

CMS (Cable Management System) – A system used to organise, support, and protect electrical cables and wiring in buildings and infrastructure, ensuring safety, accessibility, and compliance with regulations.

D

Direct Entry – Entering the construction industry without formal training or apprenticeships, often starting as a labourer.

Designer (Construction) – A professional responsible for the planning and design of buildings and structures.

E

ECS (Electrotechnical Certification Scheme) Card – A certification for electricians proving competency in electrical installation and safety.

Estimator – A construction professional who calculates the costs of materials, labour, and time required for a project.

Electrician – A skilled tradesperson who installs, maintains, and repairs electrical systems in buildings.

Engineer (Construction) – A professional who applies scientific and mathematical principles to the design and execution of construction projects.

F

Fire Safety Regulations – UK laws governing fire prevention, escape routes, and protection measures in buildings.

First Fix & Second Fix – Terms used in carpentry and electrical work:

First Aider – A trained individual responsible for providing immediate medical assistance on-site in case of injuries or emergencies, ensuring compliance with health and safety regulations.

Fall Arrest System – A safety system used to stop a worker from hitting the ground in case of a fall from height.

G

General Labourer – An entry-level construction worker who assists skilled tradespeople by performing basic tasks such as lifting, digging, and site cleaning.

Groundworker – A construction worker who prepares the foundation of a building, including drainage, paving, and excavation work.

H

Health & Safety at Work Act (1974) – The main UK law ensuring workplace safety, including construction sites.

Highways Engineer – A specialist in road construction, maintenance, and infrastructure projects.

Hot Works Permit – A permit required for any construction work involving open flames, welding, grinding, or other ignition sources to ensure fire safety measures are in place.

I

Infrastructure – Large-scale construction projects, such as roads, bridges, railways, and public utilities.

Inspector (Building/Site Inspector) – A professional responsible for ensuring construction work complies with regulations and safety standards.

IPAF (International Powered Access Federation) Qualification – A certification for operating Mobile Elevated Work Platforms (MEWPs) like scissor lifts and boom lifts. Holders receive a PAL (Powered Access Licence) card, proving competence in safe working at height.

J

Joinery – The craft of making wooden structures, such as doors, stairs, and cabinets.

L

Lifting Operations and Lifting Equipment Regulations (LOLER) – UK regulations ensuring the safe use of lifting equipment on construction sites.

Lone Working – Working alone without direct supervision, requiring additional safety measures to minimise risks.

M

Mechanical & Electrical (M&E) – A construction sector specializing in mechanical and electrical engineering within buildings.

MEP (Mechanical, Electrical, and Plumbing) – The sector of construction focused on mechanical (HVAC), electrical systems, and plumbing installations, essential for building functionality and compliance.

Method Statement – A written document detailing how specific construction tasks will be carried out safely.

N

NVQ (National Vocational Qualification) – A work-based qualification proving competency in a specific construction trade or profession.

NAPIT (National Association of Professional Inspectors & Testers) – A UK certification body for electricians, ensuring competency in inspection, testing, and certification of electrical work.

P

Painter & Decorator – A skilled worker responsible for painting, wallpapering, and finishing surfaces in buildings.

PAT (Portable Appliance Testing) – A process of inspecting electrical equipment to ensure it is safe for use.

Plasterer – A tradesperson who applies plaster to walls and ceilings to create smooth surfaces.

Plumber – A skilled worker who installs and repairs water supply, drainage, and heating systems.

PTS (Personal Track Safety) Card – A certification required for anyone working on or near railway tracks in the UK.

Project Manager (Construction) – A professional overseeing construction projects, ensuring they are completed on time and within budget.

PPE (Personal Protective Equipment) – Safety gear worn by construction workers to protect against hazards on-site. This includes helmets, high-visibility vests, safety boots, gloves, eye protection, and hearing protection. PPE is mandatory on most UK construction sites under Health & Safety regulations.

Permit to Work (PTW) – A formal safety control document required for high-risk construction tasks, such as confined space work, electrical installations, and hot works.

PASMA (Prefabricated Access Suppliers' and Manufacturers' Association) Qualification – Certification for the safe assembly, use, and dismantling of mobile access towers used in construction and maintenance work.

Q

Quantity Surveyor (QS) – A professional responsible for managing the financial and contractual aspects of a construction project.

QS (Qualified Supervisor - Electrical) – A certified individual responsible for overseeing and ensuring that all electrical installation work complies with regulations. This role is required under NICEIC, NAPIT, and other electrical certification bodies in the UK. A QS must be competent in electrical testing, inspection, and signing off work under BS 7671 (Wiring Regulations).

R

Railway Engineer – A specialist in designing and maintaining railway infrastructure, including tracks, bridges, and tunnels.

Renewable Energy Construction – The sector focusing on sustainable construction methods and energy-efficient buildings.

RAMS (Risk Assessment & Method Statement) – A document combining risk assessment and work procedures, detailing potential hazards and how to manage them safely.

Risk Assessment – A systematic process of identifying hazards, evaluating risks, and implementing control measures to ensure safety on construction sites. Required by health and safety regulations.

S

Site Manager – A professional responsible for overseeing daily operations on a construction site.

Site Supervisor – A person who assists the site manager in ensuring work is carried out correctly and safely.

SMSTS (Site Management Safety Training Scheme) – A CITB qualification for site managers covering health and safety regulations.

SSSTS (Site Supervisor Safety Training Scheme) – A CITB qualification for site supervisors covering essential safety requirements.

Subcontractor – A company or individual hired by a contractor to complete a specific part of a construction project.

Safe Isolation – A critical electrical safety procedure ensuring that circuits and equipment are completely disconnected from the power supply before maintenance or installation work. It involves proving the circuit is dead, locking off the supply, and using an approved voltage tester to verify no live current is present. Safe Isolation is essential for preventing electric shock hazards and is a key requirement under BS 7671 Wiring Regulations.

T

Telehandler Operator – A worker licensed to operate a telescopic handler for moving heavy loads on construction sites.

Tender – A formal bid submitted by contractors to win a construction project.

Traffic Marshall (Banksman) – A certified worker responsible for directing vehicle and plant movements on construction sites.

TBT (Toolbox Talk) – A short, informal safety meeting held before work begins to discuss hazards, procedures, and best practices on-site.

Task Briefing – A short, structured meeting before work begins, outlining specific tasks, safety measures, and responsibilities to ensure everyone understands the job requirements and risks.

U

Utilities in Construction – Services such as electricity, water, gas, and telecommunications installed in buildings and infrastructure projects.

W

White Card (CSCS Test Pass Certificate) – Proof that a worker has passed the CSCS health and safety test, required before applying for a CSCS card. Work at Height Regulations (2005) – UK legislation governing safety requirements for working at height in construction.

Welfare Facilities – Mandatory amenities on construction sites, including toilets, drinking water, changing rooms, and rest areas, as required by UK law.

WPP (Work Package Plan) – A document outlining safe working methods, risks, and control measures for specific construction tasks, commonly used in rail and infrastructure projects.

Research Sources & References

This section provides a comprehensive list of the key sources and references utilised throughout this book, offering readers direct access to authoritative information on various aspects of the UK construction industry.

Government and Regulatory Bodies

Construction Industry Scheme (CIS)
An HM Revenue and Customs (HMRC) initiative outlining tax requirements for contractors and subcontractors in the construction sector.
https://www.gov.uk/what-is-the-construction-industry-scheme

Health and Safety Executive (HSE)– Construction
Provides guidance on health and safety regulations specific to the construction industry.
https://www.hse.gov.uk/construction/index.htm

Common Minimum Standards for Construction

Sets out mandatory standards for government construction projects in the UK.
https://www.gov.uk/government/publications/common-minimum-standards-for-construction

National Regulation: Construction Products

Information on the regulation of construction products in the UK.
https://www.gov.uk/guidance/national-regulation-construction-products

Professional Organisations

Construction Industry Council (CIC)

A representative forum for professional bodies, research organisations, and specialist business associations in the UK construction industry.

https://www.cic.org.uk/

Construction Skills Certification Scheme (CSCS)

The leading skills certification scheme within the UK construction industry, providing proof that individuals have the necessary training and qualifications.
https://www.cscs.uk.com/

Royal Institution of Chartered Surveyors (RICS) – Construction Standards Collaborates globally to set standards in construction and infrastructure, focusing on cost management and project planning.

https://www.rics.org/profession-standards/rics-standards-and-guidance/sector-standards/construction-standards

Industry News and Resources

Construction News

A leading resource for UK construction industry news, contract wins, top contractors and clients, market intelligence, and forecasts.
https://www.constructionnews.co.uk/

Building Magazine

Provides the latest news, expertise, and intelligence from the UK building industry.

https://www.building.co.uk/

UK Construction Online

Offers news, contracts, and site reports across the UK construction sector.
https://www.ukconstructionmedia.co.uk/

Standards and Regulations

Building Regulations for England – NHBC

Information on building regulations applicable to most new buildings and many alterations of existing buildings in England and Wales.

https://www.nhbc.co.uk/builders/products-and-services/techzone/building-regs-england

Standards in the Construction Industry – Designing Buildings Wiki

An overview of the building regulations establishing minimum standards in construction.

https://www.designingbuildings.co.uk/wiki/Standards_in_the_construction_industry

Building Act 1984
An Act consolidating previous legislation concerning the construction process and related matters in England and Wales.

https://en.wikipedia.org/wiki/Building_Act_1984

Health and Safety

Building and Construction Safety Regulations and Standards
A comprehensive guide to key safety regulations and standards required for construction sites in the UK.

https://www.safesitefacilities.co.uk/knowledge-base/building-and-construction-safety-regulations-and-standards

Construction Law – HSE
Provides statutory instruments for UK legislation within the construction industry.

https://www.hse.gov.uk/construction/resources/law.htm

Economic and Statistical Data

Office for National Statistics (ONS) – Construction Industry
Offers articles and data on price movements in construction materials, productivity, and other relevant statistics.

https://www.ons.gov.uk/businessindustryandtrade/constructionindustry

Bonus

Find Your Next Construction Job Faster!

Get instant access to a list of 160 construction recruitment agencies, sorted by city and specialisation!

Scan the QR Code Below to Download

What You'll Get:

Top 160 agencies across the UK (London, Manchester, Birmingham, Scotland, Wales & more!)
Specialised recruiters for rail, civil engineering, M&E, trades, and more.
Direct contacts – websites, phone numbers, and specialisations

Choose between a printable PDF or an interactive Google Sheet

About the Author:

Daniel Szczesny is a highly experienced M&E Manager with over 25 years in the construction industry, specialising in electrical and mechanical systems across domestic, commercial, and industrial sectors.
With a strong focus on quality assurance, compliance, and project management, he has played a key role in major infrastructure projects, particularly within the rail sector, including London Underground, DLR, and Network Rail.
Daniel's expertise lies in construction management, testing, and inspection, ensuring projects meet the highest standards of safety, efficiency, and technical precision.
As an industry professional, he has worked as a Technician, Supervisor, Construction, M&E Manager, and Quality Assurance Team Leader, leading multidisciplinary teams to deliver complex construction projects on time and within budget.
Daniel firmly believes that successful project delivery is built on teamwork, respect, and strong collaboration.
He is passionate about mentoring and workforce development, fostering a learning culture where teams can enhance their technical knowledge and grow professionally. His approach emphasises integrating teams effectively, ensuring every worker feels valued and engaged in achieving common project goals.

This book is a reflection of his extensive industry experience, designed to guide newcomers through the pathways, challenges, and opportunities of a successful career in construction.

Want to connect? For more construction career insights and industry updates, feel free to reach out:
Email: daniel@constructionitis.com
Website: www.constructionitis.com
LinkedIn: linkedin.com/in/dan-szczesny-244159341

Printed in Dunstable, United Kingdom

78067761R00070